KIT CARSON

He Led the Way

Patricia Calvert

 **Marshall Cavendish**
Benchmark
New York

For
Stefan William Clarkowski—
welcome to the world!

Marshall Cavendish Benchmark
99 White Plains Road
Tarrytown, NY 10591-9001
www.marshallcavendish.us

Library of Congress Cataloging-in-Publication Data

Calvert, Patricia.
Kit Carson : he led the way / by Patricia Calvert.
p. cm. — (Great explorations)
Summary: "An examination of the life and frontier explorations of legendary trapper and Indian agent Christopher 'Kit' Carson"—Provided by publisher.
Includes bibliographical references and index.
ISBN-13: 978-0-7614-2223-5
ISBN-10: 0-7614-2223-4
1. Carson, Kit, 1809–1868—Juvenile literature. 2. Pioneers—West (U.S.)—Biography—Juvenile literature. 3. Scouts and scouting—West (U.S.)—Biography—Juvenile literature. 4. Soldiers—West (U.S.)—Biography—Juvenile literature. 5. West (U.S.)—Biography—Juvenile literature. 6. West (U.S.)—History—To 1848—Juvenile literature. 7. Frontier and pioneer life—West (U.S.)—Juvenile literature. I. Title. II. Series.

F592.C33C34 2007
978'.02092—dc22

2005037375

Photo research by Anne Burns Images

Cover photo: North Wind Picture Archives
Cover inset: North Wind Picture Archives

The photographs in this book are used by permission and through the courtesy of: *Granger Collection*: 6, 20, 24, 62, 68. *New Mexico State Records Center and Archives*: 10 (no.063893). *North Wind Picture Archives*: 12, 23, 29, 33, 50, 53, 61, 70. *Image Works*: 15, SSPL. *Denver Public Library*: 19, 88. *Colorado Historical Society*: 27, 37, 65. *Corbis*: 31, Owaki-Kulla; 38, Historical Picture Archive; 39, Joshua Strong/US Air Force. *New Mexico State University Library, Archives and Special Collections*: 34. *National Park Service*: 43. *Art Resource*: 45, National Portrait Gallery, Smithsonian Institution. *Palace of the Governors*: 47, 75, 80. *Taos Historic Museums*: 49, 56,72 (left & right), 73 (left & right), 77, 82, 84. *University of Southern California*: 54. *Kansas State Historical Society*: 87.

Printed in China
1 3 5 6 4 2

Contents

foreword

English colonists had hardly settled along parts of North America's east coast when the unknown lands to the west tugged at their imagination. The settlers had possessed enough courage to leave their homes in the Old World; now they wondered what lay beyond the forests and mountains that spread to the west.

After the Revolutionary War ended in 1783, a nation free of English rule was established. Men were able to explore the lands that had come under the new young government's control. In April 1803 Thomas Jefferson, third president of the United States, purchased 830,000 square miles (2,150,000 square kilometers) of land called the Louisiana Territory from France for $15 million. With the stroke of a pen, the fledgling nation doubled in size. On May 14, 1804, Jefferson sent an expedition headed by Meriwether Lewis and William Clark up the Missouri River to discover if a direct route—a Northwest Passage—

could be found that led all the way to the Pacific Ocean.

No such passage existed, but Lewis and Clark *did* get all the way to the Oregon coast. What they discovered on their 7,000-mile (11,270-kilometer) journey was a vast wilderness with creeks and streams inhabited by beaver, mink, and otter. News of this discovery ignited the interest of fur traders who were ever on the lookout for a new source of such a valuable commodity. During the early 1800s, furs—beaver furs in particular—were worth their weight in gold. Well-dressed gentlemen in cities of the East and in Europe paid large sums for tall sleek hats made of beaver fur that were popular at the time.

In 1807 Manuel Lisa, a fur trader from Saint Louis, was the first to take a party of trappers into the region that Lewis and Clark had described in their journals. In 1808 John Jacob Astor founded the American Fur Company and became one of the country's richest men. By 1823 advertisements for recruiting trappers appeared in newspapers around the country:

> *To Enterprising Young Men: The subscriber wishes to engage ONE HUNDRED MEN to ascend the Missouri River to its source . . . to be employed for one, two or three years.*

The salary offered—$200 for a year's hard work—meant that company owners got rich while trappers died broke. Yet men for whom the comforts of civilization held few charms responded to such invitations. Jim Bridger, Jim Beckwourth, Jedediah Smith, and hordes of others headed west to trap beaver in regions that were once known only to Native Americans or a few early French and British trappers. Such hardy adventurers were called the Mountain Men because they spent their lives in the wilderness far from towns or cities.

Tales of their exploits soon traveled far and wide. In 1826 a fifteen-year-old boy from Franklin, Missouri, listened to stories told by his older

When Kit Carson was a boy, his older brothers told him exciting stories of the exploits of the Mountain Men. In 1826, when he was fifteen years old, Kit made up his mind that that was exactly what he wanted to be.

COURAGE: A FAMILY TRAIT

Alexander Carson, Kit's great-grandfather, was a Presbyterian minister from Dumfriesshire, Scotland, who immigrated to England in the 1700s. He settled at Bradninch near a Quaker family named Boone. Like Carson, the Boones were persecuted because of their religion. In 1717 George Boone—grandfather of another American hero, Daniel—struck out with his sons for the New World, where religious freedom was tolerated, and acres of land awaited those willing to claim them. A few years later, Alexander Carson followed with his own four sons—John, Samuel, William, and James. They settled in Lancaster County, Pennsylvania, not far from the Boones. By 1761 William Carson—Kit's grandfather—had moved farther west to claim land near Wind Creek in the Shenandoah Valley.

brothers about trapping and hunting in the West. Kit Carson was small for his age, freckled, and sandy haired. When he thought about his future, he was certain of one thing: he wanted to be a Mountain Man. Kit's story—as the boy grew into a man—is a story of the American West itself, a tale punctuated by the names of places that ring with poetry: the Wind River Mountains; the *Jornada del Muerto* (Journey of Death) desert; and the Sweetwater and Powder rivers.

Kit Carson described many of his adventures in his own words. In 1856 he dictated his life story to twenty-nine-year-old John Mostin, a former U.S. Army lieutenant. For although Kit could sign his name, he could neither read nor write. Three years later, Mostin died unexpectedly, and the handwritten document disappeared. It was rediscovered in 1905 in Paris, France, in a trunk of old papers that were about to be burned. The manuscript is now owned by the Newberry Library in Chicago and was published in 1926 as part of a volume titled *Kit Carson's Own Story of His Life.*

During his years in the West, Kit Carson had been a trapper, hunter, explorer, scout, courier, soldier, and Indian agent. He had been a foe of Native Americans—most notably the Sioux, Blackfeet, Apache, Ute, and Navajo—but spent his final years as an advocate for the people he once called enemies. He set out simply to be a Mountain Man, but the appearance of his name today on mountain passes, parks, cities, and highways throughout the West is proof that Kit Carson became much more.

O N E

Runaway Boy— One Penny Reward

. . . a boy about sixteen years old . . . ran away. . . . One cent reward will be given to any person who will bring back said boy.
—The *Missouri Intelligencer*, October 6, 1826

In December 1809 the cabin along Tate's Creek in Madison, Kentucky, was filled to the rafters with Lindsey Carson's family of ten children. After his wife Lucy died in 1793, Lindsey struggled to raise their five children—William, Andrew, Moses, Sarah, and Sophie—on his own. Three years later he married Rebecca Robinson, who eventually presented him with five new children—Elizabeth, Nancy, Matilda, Robert, and Hamilton.

Lindsey, formerly a captain in the Revolutionary Army, had built the cabin on Tate's Creek himself. It provided snug shelter: three rooms with puncheon floors (thick, smooth slabs of wood fitted close together), hand-split shingles on the roof, and a stone fireplace for cooking and heat. In winter the window openings were covered with oiled paper. A ladder led to a loft where the older children slept. Lindsey and his half-grown sons made a living cutting logs and floating them downstream to New Orleans for sale. They also kept cattle and pigs, planted corn, hunted, and did a little trapping on the side.

On Christmas Eve, 1809—so near midnight it was almost Christmas Day—Rebecca Carson presented the family with a new baby. The birth came two months early, explaining why the infant was so small. The boy, number eleven in the order of children, was named Christopher, but because of his size was called Kit from the beginning. His brothers were tall, husky men, but Kit—called "the runt" by his father—stood 5 feet 5 inches (1.65 meters) tall when full grown and weighed about 140 pounds (64 kilograms).

Kentucky in the early 1800s was a wonderful place for a child to grow up. Fields had been cleared and planted with crops, but the surrounding woods were still thick with deer, elk, and bear. Creeks were full of fish; geese, ducks, and pigeons darkened the sky as

People who had heard of Kit Carson's exploits and reputation were often surprised when meeting him in person, shocked at his small size and stature.

they passed overhead. But as greater numbers of colonists poured into Kentucky, game became scarcer and disputes arose over land claims. Soon homesteaders turned their eyes farther west.

In October 1811, Lindsey Carson sold his homestead on Tate's Creek and followed the Boone family to what became the state of Missouri. The older Carson boys rode horseback; the older girls and half-grown children walked beside ox carts piled with pots, pans, and bedding; the smallest children perched on top of the load. Rebecca rode horseback and held Kit, not yet two years old, on the saddle in front of her. Kit later joked that the long ride to Missouri at such a young age left him bow-legged for life.

One of the first playthings Kit got after arriving in Missouri was a toy rifle one of his brothers whittled from a piece of wood. When Kit was four, he got a different sort of gift: a baby sister, Mary Ann, who became his favorite playmate and remained a loyal friend after they were grown. At age eight, Lindsey gave his son a real rifle, but it was their neighbor—Daniel Boone, more than eighty years old at the time—who taught Kit how to use it.

During the period of America's western settlement, the country's native population—Indians of many tribes—followed two main courses of action: they either tried to get along with white settlers or they made war on them. One of the first experiences Kit had with Indians was on a June day as he was playing at the river's edge. He noticed several pairs of bright dark eyes watching him from nearby bushes. Kit motioned to the boys to come closer. Kit knew no Indian words, and the Indian boys knew no English. So Kit pointed to himself and said his name, once, twice, three times. Soon the boys did the same. Using sign language, Kit taught them games he played with his brothers; in turn his Indian friends taught him a game played with sticks.

Not all encounters with Indians were as peaceful, however, and the Carson children always had to be on the alert. "When we went any

Daniel Boone was a longtime friend of the Carson family. When Kit was eight years old, his father gave him a rifle, but it was eighty-year-old Daniel Boone who taught Kit how to shoot it.

distance away from our house," reported Mary Ann, "we would carry bits of red cloth with us to drop if we were captured . . . so our people could trace us." She added, "I always felt completely safe when Kit was on guard duty, even when he was a boy."

Rebecca Carson had high aspirations for her children, especially for Kit. He had an exceptional memory, and she hoped he would one day become a lawyer. None of the older Carson boys attended school regularly, but Kid did for a brief time. Yet for most boys of his era, formal education held little appeal. Hunting, trapping, and defending your home were more exciting than sitting at a desk. Kit later described how his schooling ended abruptly, in third grade. "I was a young boy in the

GATEWAY TO THE WEST

The Santa Fe Trail was a dusty path across the Kansas plains, north along the Arkansas River, and over Raton Pass into New Mexico. It wasn't used by homesteaders seeking cheap land, as was the famous Oregon Trail that was established twenty years later. Rather it was a trade route into what had been Spanish territory. Until Mexico won independence from Spain in 1821, Americans weren't welcome in the area. Then in 1822 William Becknell left Franklin, Missouri, with three wagons loaded with goods. He sold his wares for six times what he had invested, earning him the nickname Father of the Santa Fe Trail. Other traders quickly followed Becknell's example, providing the developing frontier with a valuable new commercial route.

school house when the cry came, 'Indians!' I jumped for my rifle and threw down my spelling book, and there it lies."

When Kit was nine, tragedy struck the Carsons. While sixty-four-year-old Lindsey was clearing a field by burning off some timber, a flaming tree limb struck him, killing him instantly. A week later, September 11, 1818, Rebecca gave birth to another son and named him after his father. It became Kit's and his older brothers' job to plow the fields and plant and harvest the crops. Farm animals also had to be cared for, and wild game was needed for extra meat. Trapping became a way to earn extra cash to buy items the family couldn't afford otherwise.

Rebecca Carson was a widow for four years, then married Joseph Martin who had several children of his own. Soon new babies began to arrive. Thirteen-year-old Kit, usually an agreeable boy, resented his stepfather's attempts at discipline. Kit became hard to handle and was sent to live with his oldest half-brother, William, on a nearby farm. Kit wasn't any happier living under his brother's thumb. William became exasperated and made Kit the ward of a neighbor, John Ryland, who later became a Missouri supreme court judge.

In 1824, when Kit was fifteen, Ryland—believing he was acting in the boy's best interest—apprenticed him to David Workman, a saddle maker in nearby Franklin, Missouri. Saddle making was a worthy trade at a time when men on the move needed a well-outfitted horse, but Mary Ann remembered Kit's lack of enthusiasm for the job: "The only use he had for a saddle was on a horse's back."

Working in a saddle shop produced an unintended outcome. The town of Franklin was located at the head of the Santa Fe Trail. David Workman's shop became a favorite stopping-off point for trappers and traders headed to Santa Fe where beaver pelts sold for high prices and other goods often were exchanged at a 200 percent profit. After Mexico won its independence from Spain, the entire Southwest beckoned to men for whom the lure of furs, trade, and adventure was irresistible.

Among those who found the Santa Fe Trail irresistible were Kit's older brothers Andrew and Robert. In 1825 they went west with a surveying crew, and when they returned told grand tales about their adventures. Moses Carson, who had joined the Missouri Fur Company even earlier, in 1819, had already filled Kit's head with stories about the Mountain Men and their exploits. In 1826, when Andrew and Robert

Kit Carson was apprenticed to a saddle maker in Franklin, Missouri, when he was fifteen years old. Saddle making was an honorable trade, yet Kit hated being confined indoors day after day and longed for a freer life.

prepared to leave Franklin with a caravan headed for Independence, Missouri, 100 miles (161 kilometers) away, Kit begged to go along.

To Kit's dismay, his mother refused to give him permission to leave, yet the boy couldn't help but listen to the stories that were told at the saddle shop, and for him the appeal of life in the West didn't fade. Kit's apprenticeship grew more irksome as day after day he sat hunched over a wooden saddle frame, a pile of leather at his side, an awl in his fist. Finally, Kit made a decision. This time he didn't seek anyone's approval.

"In August 1826, I had the fortune to hear of a party bound [for the mountains] . . . and, without any difficulty, I was permitted to join them," Kit explained in his memoir. His absence didn't go unnoticed, but it was October 6, 1826, before David Workman posted a notice in Franklin's newspaper, the *Missouri Intelligencer*, as was required by law:

> *Notice to whom it may concern: THAT CHRISTOPHER CARSON, a boy about 16 years old, small for his age, but thick set, light hair, ran away from the subscriber . . . to whom he had been bound to learn the saddler's trade . . . on or about the first of September. . . . All persons are notified not to harbor, support or assist said boy under the penalty of the law. One cent reward will be given to any person who will bring back the said boy.*

David Workman waited a month before posting a notice of the boy's disappearance, then offered a mere penny for his return. He sympathized with Kit's decision, which had a surprising effect on his employer. In May 1827, nine months after Kit left Franklin, Workman hung a "Closed" sign on the door of his saddle shop, then headed down the Santa Fe Trail himself.

T W O

Too Young, Too Small, Too Green

*Having heard so many tales of life in the mountains . . . I concluded
to leave. . . . If I remained [in the saddle shop] I would have to pass
my life in labor that was distasteful to me.*

—Kit Carson

Kit had often heard his brothers Robert, Andrew, and Moses speak
admiringly of trader Charles Bent, who later became the first governor
of the territory of New Mexico. Kit decided to ask for a job. Bent hired
him, unconcerned with Kit's age because Bent's own brother William,
a few months younger than Kit, already was a member of the caravan
headed for Santa Fe. Other men with the wagon train recognized Kit
as the quiet, small-for-his-age kid they had seen in Workman's saddle
shop. They knew the older Carson brothers as fine horsemen who were
skilled with their rifles. So, although Kit looked "too young, too small,
too green," he was accepted among them.

Kit's first job was as a "cavvy," one of several riders who managed the *caballada*, a large herd of horses and mules that accompanied the caravan. Extra animals were always brought along to replace ones that ran off, were not strong enough to complete the journey, or were stolen by Indians. Part of a cavvy's job was to keep the herd from wandering onto the prairie where wild grass grew taller than a man's head, making it impossible to round them all up again.

The heavy wooden-wheeled vehicles in the caravan were loaded with goods that Bent intended to sell in Santa Fe: calico, linen, and velvet; buttons, thread, and scissors; pots, pans, and coffee grinders; shovels, hoes, and axes—plus a few cases of whiskey and wine.

As the caravan threaded its way across Kansas, autumn was in full swing. The skies were brilliantly blue; the grass covering the prairie had ripened to red-gold. At night the sky was studded with stars brighter than diamonds. Exposure to sights like these was one of the reasons Kit never expressed any regret about leaving Franklin. Until the end of his life, the outdoors was where he felt most at home.

The food allotment for each man on the two-month journey consisted of 50 pounds (22.7 kilograms) of flour, 50 pounds of bacon, 20 (9) of sugar, 10 (4.5) of coffee, and some salt. Beans and crackers were included as luxuries. If a man used tobacco, as Kit did, he supplied his own. Fresh meat, usually buffalo or deer, was brought to camp as needed by men that Bent hired specifically to hunt.

At night the wagons were arranged in a circle. An opening was left so the horse herd could be driven inside in case of an Indian attack. The men hobbled (tied a rope around the front legs of each horse just above the hooves) their regular mounts for grazing, and all the horses were guarded through the night by men who stood watch in two-hour shifts to protect the animals against Indians or wolves. Campfires were built outside the circle of wagons, and the men didn't linger in the firelight because it made them easy targets for Indian arrows. In summer,

THE BENT BROTHERS

Charles Bent, a founder of Bent's fort along the Arkansas River in Colorado, became Kit Carson's lifelong friend. In 1846 he was appointed the first U.S. governor of the territory of New Mexico but was assassinated three months later.

Judge Silas Bent of Saint Louis raised eleven children in a style that would have astonished a boy like Kit. The judge's large house, its veranda overlooking the Missouri River, was surrounded on three sides by apple orchards and plum trees, green lawns, and rich fields. Slaves waited on the family; the stables were full of horses descended from famous bloodlines; the kennels housed well-bred hunting dogs. The judge managed to keep seven of his children close by in Saint Louis, but four sons—Charles, William, George, and Robert—preferred life along the Santa Fe Trail.

In 1790 the U.S. population was 3.9 million; by 1850 immigration mostly from Europe had increased the nation's numbers to about 23.1 million. Hunger for land drove countless people west in search of a better life.

tents were rarely used; the men simply stretched out on the ground, rolled themselves in their blankets, and used their saddles as pillows.

One evening, when the caravan was camped along a bend in the Arkansas River, a mule driver named Andrew Broadus saw a wolf nearby. He reached for his rifle but hastily grabbed it muzzle-first. It fired, the lead ball striking him in the right arm. For several days he "suffered greatly from the effects of the wound," Kit recalled, then "his arm began to mortify," or became gangrenous. There was only one way to save Broadus's life: the arm had to be amputated.

No doctor was available, so members of the wagon team performed the grim but life-saving surgery. The patient was given whiskey to dull his pain. A knife was honed to a razor's edge. The teeth of a handsaw were sharpened with a file. After the limb was amputated,

THE SANTA FE TRAIL

Platte River

MISSOURI

Independence

COLORADO

KANSAS

Arkansas River

SANGRE DE CRISTO MOUNTAINS

Bent's Fort

OKLAHOMA

Canadian River

Taos

Santa Fe

N

NEW MEXICO

0   50   100   150 mi

Between 1821 and 1880, the Santa Fe Trail was used mostly as a trade route connecting Missouri with the present-day state of New Mexico.

the stump of Broadus's arm was cauterized (burned) with "a red hot bolt of one of the wagons . . . a plaster of tar was taken from off the wheel of a wagon" to further seal the wound. The next day, Broadus continued the journey, becoming "perfectly well before our arrival in New Mexico," Kit reported.

As the tallgrass prairie gave way to short-grass plains, the caravan ran into huge herds of buffalo, called *cibola* by the Spanish. At first glance the grass looked dead, yet it was so nutritious it was eaten greedily by the massive brown beasts as they put on layers of fat for the winter. If several buffalo were killed at the same time, it was impossible to eat all the meat before it started to rot, so it was preserved Indian-style, by drying. It was sliced into thin strips and hung on the sides of the wagons to dehydrate in the sun as the caravan moved along. It was then stacked inside the wagons and later used in soups or stews.

In November 1826 the caravan halted a few miles outside Santa Fe. According to custom, a couple of men were sent ahead to make trade arrangements with Mexican customs officials, while those who stayed behind cleaned up the wagons and polished harnesses and saddle gear. Then the men washed their faces, slicked down their hair, and put on the cleanest clothes they had before entering the city. The caravan was the largest to arrive in Santa Fe and caused a great stir. Cries of "*Los Americanos, los carros!*"—"The Americans, the caravans!"—rang out, a welcome in a foreign tongue that probably startled the boy from Workman's saddle shop. After the goods were sold, Kit collected his pay, then realized he needed another job. He soon learned that a group of traders was heading for Taos, 80 miles (129 kilometers) north of Santa Fe, high in the Sangre de Cristo (Blood of Christ) Mountains. They needed a cavvy, and he signed on. By the first week of December they arrived in Taos, then the third-largest city in New Mexico with a population of almost four thousand.

At 7,000 feet (11,270 kilometers), the winters in Taos were cold and

Beginning in 1822 covered wagons loaded with trade goods—pots and pans, axes and shovels, cotton cloth and thread—made the long journey to Santa Fe, where the items could be sold for huge profits.

sometimes snowy. The houses were made of adobe (clay bricks), their 3- to 6-foot-thick (0.9- to 1.8-meters-thick) walls keeping them warm in winter and cool in summer. The ceilings were made of *vigas*, or peeled logs, then the roofs were covered with dirt. The citizens of Taos called themselves the People of the Red Willows, because the trees

In December 1826, several days shy of his sixteenth birthday, Kit Carson first entered Taos, New Mexico. The houses that made up the growing town were built of adobe or clay bricks and had walls 3 to 6 feet (0.9 to 1.8 meters) thick, which helped keep the residents warm in winter and cool in summer.

growing beside a stream that cut through the town turned bright red in autumn.

When Kit entered the city that November day, he could not have foreseen that he would call Taos home for the next forty-two years. Nor did he expect to run into an old family friend as he tried to figure out his next course of action. Matthew Kincaid had served with Lindsey Carson in the Missouri militia and invited Kit to spend the winter at his cabin a few miles from Taos. It proved to be a busy time. Kincaid, who spoke Spanish as well as several Indian dialects, taught Kit what he knew. They also hunted buffalo and trapped, and Kit put to use the skills he had learned in the saddle shop. He made leggings, moccasins, and jackets from the buffalo hides, trimming the jackets with long fringe. The fringe wasn't merely for decoration; in an emergency it could be cut off and used to mend a moccasin or repair a bridle.

When the grass turned green in the spring of 1827, Kit joined a caravan headed back to the States. At the Arkansas River he ran into several trappers headed in the opposite direction who urged him to return with them to New Mexico. He did, confident he would again find lodging with Kincaid. Kincaid, however, had died unexpectedly, and Kit found himself without a place to live. He moved on to El Paso as the driver of a mule team, earning a dollar a day. In a short time he was out of work again and returned to Taos.

Ewing Young, a well-known trapper originally from Knox County, Tennessee, had just opened a store in Taos to outfit trappers headed into the mountains. It was Kit's aim to be a trapper himself, so he approached Young, hoping for a chance to get started. Instead he was offered a job for the winter months at the Taos store in exchange for room and board.

In 1828 Kit put his language skills to work and traveled with a trade caravan to Chihuahua as an interpreter for Colonel Philip Trammel. Chihuahua, the Mexican capital of the province of the same name, had a population of nearly ten thousand, yet in spite of the city's size, work again was hard to find. Kit took a job in Chihuahua's copper mines, but mining proved to be as dismal as saddle making so he quit after a few months. It had been the exciting tales of trapping and hunting that had lured him down the Santa Fe Trail, not a string of dull jobs just to make ends meet. It was time to move on, so—as became Kit's lifelong habit—that was exactly what he did.

T H R E E

Bound for California!

*A guard was placed over the tanks [deer-skin water bags] to prohibit
anyone from making use of more than his due allowance.*

—Kit Carson

In August 1829 Kit heard that Ewing Young was recruiting forty men—
Americans, Canadians, and voyageurs (French explorers) from New
Orleans—to join him on a trapping expedition to the Gila River territory.
Young, who was seventeen years older than Kit, had trapped for many
years throughout the West, and few surpassed him "in terms [of] the
sheer distance covered." Men who had worked with Young called him
"brave and daring to a fault." Young had hired Kit to work in the out-
fitter's store two years earlier, and now Kit wasted no time in approaching his former employer. Young remembered the quiet, dependable
young fellow and hired him on the spot.

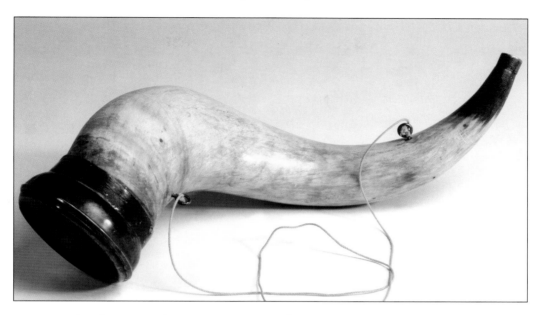

A powder horn with a strap made of rawhide that was owned by Kit Carson. Each Mountain Man was responsible for outfitting himself, including a rifle, powder, lead for bullets, a horse and saddle, and clothing.

Each man in Young's party was responsible for outfitting himself. Kit already owned a good horse whose back he protected with two *apishamores,* saddle blankets made of soft buffalo-calf skin that Kit used at the end of the day for his own bed. He carried a rifle across the saddle in front of him so it could be used at a moment's notice. He took gunpowder and lead for making bullets. He had a whetstone for sharpening a skinning knife, a cap for cold weather, and strips of an old, cut-up blanket to wrap around his feet when the weather turned bitter (socks were a luxury). He took an extra pair of moccasins and a tanned deerskin to make new ones when the old pair wore out.

There were two aspects of Young's plans that Kit knew little about. First, the Gila River lay within Mexican territory. Anglos—"Americans"—were not allowed to trap in Mexican waters because the men often sold their furs in Saint Louis, depriving the Mexican government of expected revenue. Although Americans could apply for special trapping licenses, they were difficult to get. Second, the Gila River country was occupied by Apache, who generally lived peaceably with their Mexican neighbors but despised whites and attacked them whenever possible.

Although Young knew it was illegal to trap in the beaver-rich creeks of Mexican territory, he'd learned the hard way that a license wasn't worth much. In 1828 he and a trapping partner, Milton Sublette, got a license from Governor Narbona. Trapping was good, and Young and Sublette harvested many pelts. In spite of having a license, however, Mexican officials accused the two men of trespassing. They were arrested, spent two days in jail in Taos, and their furs—worth twenty thousand dollars—were seized.

This time Young intended to deliberately deceive Mexican authorities. As he left Taos he announced that he intended to pursue some Indians who had threatened five American trappers a few months earlier. He headed north into country that belonged to the United States under the terms of the Louisiana Purchase. Mexican officials were suspicious and sent troops to follow Young as he led his forty-man party out of Taos. Several days later the troops turned back, satisfied that Young didn't intend to do any trapping. As soon as they left, Young boldly changed course and marched southwest into forbidden territory.

True to their reputation for attacking whites, the Apache descended on Young and his men at their camp along the Salt River. Young ordered everyone to hit the dirt, giving the impression that the trappers were few in number (which was true) and were afraid (which was not), thereby luring the Indians into close range. When the Apache stalked boldly into camp, the trappers opened fire. Fifteen Indians were killed, including a chief. It was Kit's first fight, and he was responsible for the death of one Apache. Although the loss of their comrades made

The mountain streams of the West contained the gold that trappers were seeking—in the form of fur-bearing animals. The water in which they trapped was typically ice cold, because the best furs were those taken in winter, when pelts were in the best condition.

the Indians cautious, it did not drive them off for good. Every night they sneaked into camp to steal horses, mules, or beaver traps.

At the Verde River in what today is central Arizona, Young divided his party. He sent one group of twenty-two men back to Taos to pick up extra traps, horses, and mules to replace those stolen by the Apache, with instructions about where to meet later. With the other eighteen, including Kit, Young set off for California—also under Mexican control—where the streams were said to be even richer with beaver. In preparation for crossing the Mojave Desert, three deer were killed. They were skinned with special care, the meat was dried, and the hides were made into water bags.

Before the trip began, Kit's knowledge of sign Indian dialects was put to use. Young sent him to a nearby Navajo village to find out the best route to take across the desert, a "country never explored before." Kit—not yet twenty years old—rode out alone, something few men would have had the courage to do. He told the Indians he came in peace and gained their trust. Then the chief of the tribe warned Kit what the Americans would face in the desert: hunting would be poor; water would be scarce; everyone would suffer terribly before they reached their destination. Nevertheless, Young's men set off the next day in high spirits, anticipating an even bigger harvest of pelts.

"The first four days' march was over a sandy country, burned up, and not a drop of water," Kit remembered. The deerskin water bags were guarded to prevent anyone from taking more than was allowed: one drink per day per man. On the fourth day, the mules were the first to detect water a mile off and hurried toward it on trembling legs. The men and their animals rested for two days beside the water hole, then the deerskin bags were refilled and the journey continued.

The Navajo chief had been right: the desert continued to torture both man and beast. Heat rose in shimmering waves as four more days' travel revealed no trace of water. The men's eyes grew red rimmed; their lips cracked; their tongues swelled. The animals suffered most, for they were deprived of even the tiny daily ration granted to the men. At last the trappers reached the lower end of the Colorado River, below the huge sandstone chasm carved during the Ice Age that today is called the Grand Canyon.

In 1829 Kit Carson joined Ewing Young's trapping party. The men, mules, and horses nearly died of thirst as they crossed the desert, but a plentiful supply of water was found at the lower end of the Grand Canyon.

Several days later Young's party arrived at the Spanish mission of San Gabriel in California, overseen by Bernardo Sanchez, a Franciscan priest. At San Gabriel, Spanish descendants supervised the labor of "one thousand Indians," Kit said, as well as "fine fields and vineyards . . . it was a paradise on earth." Ten miles (16 kilometers) to the east was a dusty village, the City of Angels, too small to arouse any curiosity in Young or his men. Today this settlement—Los Angeles—is one of the largest cities in the world, with a population of about ten million.

Young was mindful that he was a visitor in Mexican territory and was not supposed to be trapping. He let his men rest only one day at San Gabriel before traveling over the mountains, out of sight of watchful authorities. He found plenty of wild game—antelope, deer, and elk—and, even more to his liking, streams full of beaver. Young's men had hardly set their traps when they encountered other trappers—sixty-one members of Canada's Hudson Bay Company headed by Peter Skene Ogden. The two leaders were competing against each other for furs, yet Young and Skene courteously exchanged information about the area. Then Ogden headed north to the Columbia river country of present-day Oregon. For Kit, the trip to California was profitable in two ways. First, the pack mules were loaded with 1 ton (0.9 metric ton) of furs, which were sold for $12 per pound, yielding $24,000. Each man was paid his share, making him richer—briefly—than he had ever been. "We passed the time gloriously," Kit remembered, "spending our money freely, never thinking that our lives had been risked in gaining it." Second, Kit used his excellent memory to record a mental map of the country he had traveled across. It would become one of his most valuable possessions.

Charles Bent, who had given Kit his chance to travel the Santa Fe Trail after he left Workman's saddle shop, was in Taos when Kit returned in 1831 after an absence of almost two years. Bent was on his way to Saint Louis to load several wagons with goods for trade in Taos. He planned to use oxen this time, because they "wouldn't stampede like horses and mules," making it harder for the Apache to steal them. Bent offered Kit a job as an ox-team driver.

But Kit had tasted the excitement of trapping; he wanted nothing to do with driving a team, not even for Bent. Thomas Fitzpatrick, called

Kit Carson called California's Mission of San Gabriel a
paradise. It was located near the present city of Los Angeles in a
valley filled with lush meadows that were protected by
mountains to the north and south.

"Broken Hand" by the Indians, also happened to be in Taos. He was
headed north to the Platte river country and was recruiting men—Jim
Bridger among them—for the Rocky Mountain Fur Company. Kit did
not have to think twice about signing on.

In 1835 Kit Carson met Waanibe ("Singing Grass"), a young Arapaho Indian woman, at the Green River rendezvous in present-day Wyoming. He married her that summer and renamed her Alice. When their first daughter was born, he named the baby Adaline, in honor of his favorite niece.

No sooner had the trappers set up winter headquarters at the head of Idaho's Salmon River than they discovered—as John Colter had thirty years earlier—that the Blackfeet were even more hostile to whites than the Apache. Right away they "lost four or five men who were out hunting for buffalo," Kit noted in his memoir. Even so, he lived in Blackfoot country for the next ten years and came to know it like the back of his hand. "We traveled north till we struck the Platte River and then . . . trapped to the head of the Sweetwater," he recalled, "then on to Green River, and then to Jackson's Hole on a fork of the Columbia River, and from there on to the head of the Salmon River."

Bound for California!

At the Green River rendezvous in the summer of 1835, twenty-six-year-old Kit met an Arapaho girl named Waanibe, which meant "Singing Grass" in her native language. He took part in a Soup Dance, an Arapaho ceremony in which young women chose their partners. Waanibe picked him. Unknown to Kit, Chouinard, a French trapper at the rendezvous (the Americans called him Shunar) had already taken a fancy to Waanibe.

The Frenchman, 6 feet 3 inches (1.9 meters) tall, believed he was more than a match for a man nearly a foot shorter. When a quarrel broke out between them, Kit said, "I allowed him to draw his gun. We both fired at the same time . . . I shot him through the arm." Soon after, Kit married Waanibe and gave her an American name, Alice. Many Mountain Men, including Jim Bridger, Joe Meek, and Milton Sublette took Indian wives, but Kit never mentioned Alice in his memoir. Years later he admitted fearing the scorn of white society.

F O U R
Land of Many Rivers

We trapped the Yellowstone, Otter, and Musselshell rivers . . . up the Big Horn and on to the Powder River . . . [up] Twenty-Five-Yard River to the Three Forks of the Missouri, and then up the North Fork. . . .

—Kit Carson

In the autumn of 1835, Jim Bridger—a man inclined to take greater risks than Kit—decided to head into the Three Forks country of western Montana where the Madison, Gallatin, and Jefferson rivers emptied into the Missouri. The water was thick with beaver; the drawback was that although Three Forks was a trapper's paradise, it was also in the heart of Blackfoot territory. Kit joined Bridger's party but complained that a man "could hardly go a mile without being fired upon."

Trappers—called Big Knives by the Blackfeet—were despised because they competed with the Indians who also trapped beaver, mink, and otter. The Indians exchanged their pelts with the only whites they had any regard for—traders—for rifles, ammunition, and food supplies such as coffee, sugar, salt, and flour. John Kirk Townsend, who attended the Green River rendezvous with Kit, summed it up best: "The Blackfoot is a sworn and determined foe."

On September 9, the Bridger-Carson party came upon another group of trappers camped along the Madison River, who reported a recent attack by the Blackfeet. Two men had been badly wounded, and three horses had been killed and six stolen. Richard Owens, shot twice in the leg, hobbled around camp on homemade crutches. As Kit and the other trappers visited, Kit discovered that he and Owens shared a similar history. Owens, three years younger, had been apprenticed to a gunsmith. By age sixteen he was expert at building and repairing rifles. Then, like Kit, he had set out for the wilderness. The two men developed a friendship that lasted the rest of their lives.

Despite what had happened to Owens and his party, Carson and several companions ventured farther up the Madison to set traps. To the west the hillsides were covered with aspen groves; to the east the area was thick with pines. The region was prime trapping country, but before the men could bait their traps they were attacked by eighty Blackfeet.

After Jim Bridger's parents died, he was apprenticed to a blacksmith near Saint Louis, Missouri. Like Kit Carson, Bridger set his heart on becoming a Mountain Man. He headed west when he was eighteen years old, and in 1826 he was the first white man to see the Great Salt Lake.

The Blackfeet were the most hostile of all the mountain tribes. They called white trappers Big Knives and fiercely resented any intrusion into their territory because they were trappers themselves.

The Americans dashed for cover among the pines. Rather than waste ammunition by firing randomly at the Indians who were hidden among the aspens on the opposite hillside, Carson and the others laid low throughout the afternoon. Disgusted, the Indians finally set fire to the woods to drive the trappers into the open. Osborne Russell later recalled in his memoir, *Journal of a Trapper*, "Death seemed almost inevitable." Desperate to save themselves, the trappers kindled a backfire (a fire started in front of an advancing forest fire to stop it by creating a burned area in between) and escaped under the cover of smoke.

This was only the beginning of escalating violence between the Blackfeet and the trappers. On January 29, 1837, the Bridger-Carson

In 1837, in Montana's Three Forks region, the Blackfeet planned to attack Kit Carson's trapping party but retreated when the aurora borealis, or northern lights, turned the sky a shimmering red. The Indians believed it was a sign that they would be defeated in battle.

party set off after some Blackfeet who had attacked their group. Many Blackfeet were killed, but as the Indians retreated, carrying their dead and wounded with them, Bridger warned, "In a short time . . . five or six hundred will return" to avenge their comrades. The trappers, only sixty in number, seemed doomed, but everyone set to work building a fort with walls 6 feet (1.8 meters) high of cottonwood logs. In early February the Indians reappeared in much larger numbers than Bridger had predicted—about 1,100 strong. The night before the expected assault the weather turned bitterly cold, causing the frozen trees to crack with a sound like rifle fire. Tensions mounted as the trappers waited for dawn, the Indians' favorite time to attack.

The attack never came. At about 10 p.m., the winter sky suddenly lit up with a magnificent display of the aurora borealis—the northern lights—of brilliant blue, green, and yellow. Then to the trappers' amazement the sky turned blood red. The Blackfeet saw the change, too. Unnerved, the Indians packed up and left, for they believed the bloody color was a warning from their Great Spirit that defeat awaited them in the coming battle.

Not everything in 1837 involved fighting and death. During that year—the month was never documented—Alice gave birth to a daughter. Kit named her Adaline, in honor of a favorite niece. As a grown woman, Adaline was said to be "a dark, exotic-looking child" who resembled her Arapaho mother. With a wife and child to care for, Kit signed on to provide the men at Fort Davy Crockett, located on the western bank of the Green River, with a four-month supply of meat. The winter turned out to be "one of the coldest . . . I have ever experienced," Kit said, with snow so deep the horses could not paw through it to find grass. "We had to keep our animals in a corral. . . . Their feed was cottonwood bark, which we would pull from the trees and thaw out by the fire."

Kit was in the West to trap beaver, however, not to bring in meat for men who could not or did not want to hunt for themselves. He teamed up with four companions to head into the Black Hills region, where they trapped for three months, collecting many furs. About 1838 Kit packed up his wife and daughter and moved to Bent's Fort—named after his old friend Charles Bent—along the Arkansas River in present-day Colorado. After they were settled, Alice gave birth to a second daughter but died soon after.

Although Kit never mentioned Alice in his memoir, he later told a friend, "She was a good wife to me. I never came in . . . that she did not have warm water ready for my feet." It was a simple kindness appreciated by a man whose sockless feet were exposed to frostbite and ice-cold mountain streams. Alice's death meant Kit was left with two baby daughters and no one to care for them. He took a Cheyenne wife, but she soon objected to caring for another woman's children. She ended the marriage Indian fashion by placing Kit's belongings outside the tipi they shared.

Being the father of two motherless children was not the only problem Kit faced. "Beaver was getting very scarce," he lamented. The free-for-all fur trade was coming to an end, not only because overtrapping in streams throughout the West had resulted in declining numbers of beaver but because a change in men's fashion eliminated the demand for pelts. Gentlemen in the East as well as Europe began to wear hats made of silk rather than ones of fur.

Kit realized it was time to "try [my] hand at something else." In the autumn of 1841, he returned to Bent's Fort and found someone to look after his children. "I was kindly . . . offered employment to hunt for the fort at one dollar per day." After eight months, Kit took Adaline, about five years old, back to Missouri to live with his favorite sister, Mary Ann. The name and fate of Kit's youngest daughter have been lost to history. Did she die in infancy? Was she left in the care of her mother's people?

Once he arrived in Missouri, Kit became uncertain about how his family would accept his half-Indian child, so he left Adaline with friends while he continued on to Mary Ann's house by himself. To his relief, his family welcomed him with open arms and urged him to go back for his daughter. Adaline was enrolled in the Howard Female Seminary (a convent school) in Fayette, Missouri. Life wasn't easy for her, though, and she was called "a wild girl" during her youth. Later, Adaline married, went to California, and died while only in her twenties.

After Adaline was settled in the convent school, Kit returned to Taos. He learned that his friend Charles Bent had taken a Mexican wife, Ignacia Jaramillo, the daughter of Francisco Jaramillo, a well-respected Mexican businessman. Bent introduced Kit to his wife's younger sister, Maria Josefa, called Josefa by her family. Kit soon decided he would like to marry her, so to prepare for that possibility he converted to the Catholic faith and was baptized by Father Antonio Martinez on January 28, 1842.

BENT'S FORT

Between 1829 and 1832, Charles and William Bent built one of the most famous forts in the West, along the Arkansas River between what became modern-day Las Animas and La Junta, Colorado. Western painter George Bird Grinnell described it as a "stopping place for all travellers on the Santa Fe trail." The fort, 100 by 150 feet (30 by 46 meters)—about half the size of a football field—had adobe walls 6 feet (1.8 meters) thick at their base and 17 feet (5.2 meters) high. Its east-facing doors were made of solid planks. Inside the fort were twenty-two private rooms for visitors' convenience, a saddle shop, a gunsmith shop, and a trade store. On holidays the Bents celebrated with feasting and music. "There was always a Frenchman or two who could play the violin and guitar," wrote Grinnell. Most importantly, the Bent brothers dealt fairly with the Indians and were an important reason many Plains tribes remained friendly to whites as long as they did.

Kit took stock of his situation: he was thirty-two years old, had a daughter to support, and hoped to marry again. "It has now been sixteen years I have been in the mountains," he noted, but the fur trade had declined to the point that a man could no longer make a living as a trapper. A few of his old friends—Jim Bridger and Tom Fitzpatrick among them—had taken jobs as guides for military expeditions and

Bent's fort, located along the Arkansas River in Colorado, was a stopover for many travelers headed along the Santa Fe Trail. Inside the compound were a gunsmith's shop, a saddle shop, and a store. At holiday time, people from near and far gathered in the compound to sing, dance, and celebrate.

for caravans of settlers headed west. Should he do the same?

"Becoming tired of the settlements," Kit later recalled, "I took a steamer for the upper Missouri." Until then, he had been only one of hundreds of trappers whose names are now forgotten. His decision to take up a different challenge would inscribe the name Kit Carson in the history books of the American West.

FIVE

Change of fortune

*Colonel Fremont . . . was aboard the same boat . . . I told [him] that
I had been some time in the mountains and thought I could guide
him to any point he wished to go. . . .*

—Kit Carson

On April 25, 1842, John Charles Frémont was commissioned by the U.S.
Army Corps of Topographical Engineers to lead a party of surveyors to
map "the country between the frontiers of the Missouri and the South
Pass in the Rocky Mountains." Frémont had no experience in the West
and hired Captain Andrew Drips as a guide. When Frémont boarded a
steamer in Saint Louis for the trip up the Missouri, however, Drips was
nowhere in sight.

Kit heard of the young officer's predicament through shipboard
gossip and wasted no time in making Frémont's acquaintance. Kit's

John Charles Frémont studied mathematics in college and became a surveyor. After he married the daughter of Missouri's influential official Thomas Hart Benton, the senator made sure that Frémont was selected to lead a surveying team into the United States' unexplored western territories.

knowledge of the West was respected among trappers and traders, but he was unknown to the wider world. Frémont had no reason to trust a man he had never laid eyes on before, so he made a few inquiries. What he heard convinced him he had found the guide he needed.

Frémont considered himself a good judge of character and summed up his impression of Kit. "I was pleased with him and his manner of speaking. He was a man of medium height, broad-shouldered and deep-chested, with a clear, steady blue eye and frank speech." The friendship that began in 1842 aboard a steamship in Saint Louis continued until Kit's death.

"He told me he would engage me," Kit recalled, "paying me one hundred dollars per month." It was a princely sum; by contrast, the French voyageurs on the same expedition earned seventy-five cents a day. Kit had good reason to be interested in his wage: he had promised to pay forty dollars a month for Adaline's room and board at the convent school.

Frémont's expedition was composed of twenty-two men, mostly voyageurs, and included a German mapmaker named Charles Preuss. The steamer arrived at Chouteau's Landing on June 4, 1842, then eight carts loaded with surveying equipment were hauled to a trading post 12 miles (19.3 kilometers) away along the Kansas River. Heavy rain began to fall; the river became so swollen that crossing it seemed impossible. Nevertheless, on June 14, Frémont decided to try.

To the amazement of the voyageurs, Frémont had brought along an "India-rubber boat . . . twenty feet long and five broad." The baggage carts were loaded onto it and ferried across the river one or two at a time. It was nearly nightfall before the final crossing was made, and the boat capsized. Men leaped into the water and saved almost everything except some sugar and a bag of coffee. The loss of the coffee mattered most to Kit, for he was very fond of it. The next day Kit and one of the Frenchmen, Lucien Maxwell, were sick because of the hours they had spent in the cold water, so the journey was temporarily halted while they recovered. For Kit, the delay had an unexpected benefit: friendly Kaw Indians visited Frémont's camp and sold the expedition 30 pounds (13.6 kilograms) of coffee.

Not all of the members of Frémont's expedition were grown men. One was twelve-year-old Randolph Benton, the younger brother of Frémont's wife, Jessie. When the expedition entered Pawnee territory, members of the expedition paired up each night to guard the horse herd since the Pawnees were known to be horse thieves. The first time Randolph was scheduled to take the ten-to-midnight watch a severe thunderstorm blew in, rattling the air with thunder and splitting the sky with lightning. Frémont was pleased to report the boy "stood it out, and took [his] turn regularly afterward."

On July 8, 1842, the sight of riders in the distance alarmed Kit. He

Like Kit Carson, Lucien Maxwell, a trader from Taos, New Mexico, joined Frémont's first three expeditions. The two men became lifelong friends. Later, Maxwell became one of the largest landowners in the United States, with 1,750,000 acres (709,000 hectares) to his name.

raised his rifle, prepared to defend Frémont and the others, only to realize the approaching figures were not Indians. It was a party of traders led by his old friend Jim Bridger, who arrived with bad news. The Sioux were angry about invasions of their territory and had banded together with the Gros Ventre tribe. They had vowed to wage war on the whites wherever they were found, and Bridger warned the surveyors not to proceed.

Frémont, whose stubbornness later proved to be one of his greatest weaknesses, replied that his orders called for him to go deep into Sioux country and that was exactly what he aimed to do, or die in the attempt. Kit, who had survived many Indian attacks, disagreed with Frémont's decision, causing a brief rift in their friendship. "Carson . . . fully supported the opinion given by Bridger," Frémont noted in his official report. He was annoyed that Carson considered the danger so great that "he made his will," raising the anxiety of the other men. As it turned out, the push into Indian territory resulted in no casualties. Carson eventually admitted that Frémont's "perseverance . . . is the main cause of his success."

In early August, Frémont saw a majestic mountain peak rise out

HOW CHEERFULLY HE SUFFERED

John Charles Frémont, son of a French father and a Virginian mother, was born in 1813 in Georgia. His father died when the boy was five, and the family then moved to Charleston, South Carolina. John excelled at Latin, Greek, and mathematics in college. He also enjoyed picnics and socializing with local girls, which resulted in his dismissal for neglecting his studies. He became a part-time surveyor, then married Jessie Benton, daughter of Senator Thomas Hart Benton of Missouri. Benton, an advocate of America's westward expansion, urged Congress to select his new son-in-law to survey the unexplored territories in the West. The backing of a powerful senator did not mean Frémont expected special treatment for, as Kit remarked, "how cheerfully he suffered with his men while undergoing the severest of hardship."

HEARTBREAKING BEAUTY

Girls often married at a young age on the frontier. Maria Josefa Jaramillo was not quite fifteen years old at the time of her marriage to thirty-three-year-old Kit Carson. "Her style of beauty was of the haughty, heartbreaking kind—such as would lead a man . . . to risk his life for one smile," wrote one of Kit's friends. Fortunately, Josefa remained close to her family, especially her sister Ignacia, Charles Bent's wife, because early in their marriage Kit was gone from Taos for as long as two years at a stretch.

After three attempts in 1846, on August 15 Frémont's men finally reached the tallest peak in the Wind River Range in present-day Wyoming. Readings with modern instruments indicate that the mountain, now called Fremont's Peak, measures 13,745 feet (4,192 meters).

of Wyoming's Wind River Range and judged it to be the highest point in the Continental Divide. Since part of his mission was to measure such heights, he set out to climb to the top. (The tallest peak in the Rockies actually is Mount Elbert in Colorado, at 14,433 feet [4,402 meters].) On August 12, 1842, Frémont, Carson, Preuss, and twelve others set out with enough dried meat and coffee to last them for two days.

The first day was spent hacking a path through thick underbrush to the base of the peak. After a midday meal on August 13, the men began their upward trek. They took no coats or food because Frémont believed the climb would take only a few hours. The ascent up the "savage sublimity of naked rock" was far steeper than it appeared from a distance; the men were soon exhausted. One almost died in a fall, Frémont vomited repeatedly from altitude sickness, and the group was ultimately forced back to base camp. The following morning they set out again. The climbers encountered snowfields, suffered more altitude sickness, and turned back a second time. On August 15, however, Preuss got to the pinnacle and was able to take a barometer reading—13,570 feet (4,139 meters). Modern readings indicate the peak—now called Fremont Peak—is 13,745 feet (4,192 meters) high.

In September 1842, with Frémont no longer needing Carson's services, Kit left the expedition at Fort Laramie in Wyoming territory where some of his old trapping partners were spending the winter. For old times' sake he returned to the life he knew best: trapping. Then on his return to Taos, Kit sold his furs for what they would bring and was married to Josefa Jaramillo on February 6, 1843.

Kit had been married only a few months when he heard that Frémont was passing through New Mexico and was preparing for a second expedition. As a matter of courtesy, Kit called on his former commander but made it plain his visit "was not to seek employment." He intended to become a family man—yet when Frémont again invited Kit to act as a guide, Carson did not hesitate. The journey was all the more tempting when Kit discovered his old trapping partner Tom Fitzpatrick had already signed on.

Frémont's second expedition, also sponsored by the U.S. government, was far more ambitious than the first. It involved forty men, was scheduled to last a year, and its purpose was "to give a connected survey of the interior of our continent." But the stubborn streak that was part of Frémont's character nearly led to the failure of the entire venture. By the time the men reached the Sierra Nevada Mountains of eastern California, it was the dead of winter—January 1844. Yet Frémont, as bullheaded as ever, refused to postpone the journey until the spring thaw. The howitzer (cannon) that had been hauled along was abandoned after it became too difficult to pull it through 6-foot (1.8-meter) snowdrifts. (For years, professional and amateur treasure hunters have searched for the cannon; it has never been found.)

The ordeal of crossing the Sierras in wintertime took a dreadful toll on the expedition. When starvation threatened, Frémont ordered some mules and dogs be killed for food. When he fell into an icy stream, Kit saved his life by jumping in to drag him out. Not only were the men starving, the pack animals were suffering, too. "Driven by hunger," Kit remembered, "[the mules] had eaten one another's tails [and] the leather of the pack saddles."

In February, Frémont tried to boost the men's spirits by reminding them that Sutter's Fort was only 70 miles (113 kilometers) away. In preparation for the final push, a camp dog was killed for food, skimpy fare for men about to set out on what would be the final stretch of their horrific journey. No one expected it would take five weeks to cover those 70 miles.

Frémont's expedition began its final climb on February 2, 1844. Ten men mounted on the strongest animals went ahead to break a trail through a high mountain pass. When the man in the lead became exhausted, he and his horse traded places with the rider at the rear of the column. Sixteen miles (26 kilometers) were covered the first day. The second day was less productive because the men and animals were so worn out. Camp was pitched, then everyone rested for two weeks.

Conditions worsened when the journey was resumed. The icy snow crust slashed the horses' legs like knives. On February 28, Frémont lost a prized possession: his horse Proveau collapsed and died. Soon even the strongest animals refused to move. Then voyageur Baptiste Derosier became lost; when he staggered back into camp he was a changed man. "Hunger and fatigue . . . had crazed him," Frémont reported.

After reaching Sutter's Fort at the junction of the American and Sacramento rivers on March 6, 1844, the explorers rested for three

On Frémont's second expedition, in 1844, he refused to wait until spring to cross the Sierra Nevadas in California. In the dead of winter, it took five weeks to travel 70 miles (112.7 kilometers), an ordeal that killed Frémont's horse Proveau. Two men in the party became crazed from the hardship caused by the starvation and the excessive cold.

weeks. The effects of the ordeal left a permanent mark on a second man, who "became deranged . . . from the effects of starvation." Captain Sutter, amazed that Frémont had succeeded in crossing the Sierras in the dead of winter, fed the travelers, tended to their needs, and when they set out again he presented Frémont with a fine gift: a gray horse to replace Proveau. Frémont named it Sacramento.

By March 24, 1844, the expedition was ready to head home. Kit led the way as the men recrossed the Sierras and by April 19 cut over to the Old Spanish Trail. There had been no loss of life on the terrible first passage across the mountains, but two men died on the way home. On May 9, Indians along the Colorado River caught Baptiste Tabeau, the best liked of the voyageurs, when he went back along the trail to find a lame mule. They killed him, threw his body in the river, and stole his horse. This time, it was Kit's turn to be stubborn; he

Captain John A. Sutter arrived in California in 1839, received a land grant from the Spanish government, established a sawmill along the Sacramento River, and became a prosperous and well-respected businessman. In 1848 gold was discovered near the mill. Sutter's business was eventually ruined, and he died penniless.

insisted on avenging Tabeau's death no matter what the cost. This time, though, it was Frémont who urged caution, and the discouraged travelers pushed on. Then on May 23, tragedy struck again. As rafts were built to cross the Sevier River, Francois Badeau grabbed his rifle muzzle-first; it discharged, killing him.

On July 1, 1844, the expedition arrived at Bent's Fort. On July 4 the Bent brothers, famous for their hospitality, organized a feast for the explorers. As the men celebrated the end of their long travail, no one—Kit least of all—guessed that Frémont was already planning for a third expedition.

SIX

The Conquest of California

I told [General Stephen W. Kearny] that I could not turn back. . . . I was under more obligations to Fremont than to any other man alive.

—Kit Carson

On Christmas Eve, 1844, Josefa invited family and friends in Taos to help celebrate Kit's thirty-fifth birthday. *Luminarias* (lanterns) lit the yard, and partygoers wandered through the plaza holding *anchones*, or torches fueled by the resin from pine trees. Feasting and dancing followed, though Kit had never learned to waltz and laughed at his clumsiness.

Kit had earned $1,200 as a guide for Frémont's second expedition. Now he had enough money "to settle on some good stream" and start homesteading. In March 1845, in partnership with Dick Owens whom he had met in Montana's Three Forks country several years earlier, Kit

One of the earliest portraits of Kit Carson, from about 1845, taken at the time he first tried his hand at ranching. He went into partnership with his friend Dick Owens and settled along the Little Cimarron River east of Taos, New Mexico.

bought land along the Little Cimarron River 50 miles (81 kilometers) east of Taos. Temporary shelters were built; Josefa took charge of cooking and housekeeping; and the men put up corrals for horses, cattle, and sheep. Corn was planted—but before it could be harvested a message arrived from Bent's Fort.

Frémont, now promoted to captain, had wrangled $50,000 from Congress to conduct a third expedition. Once again he was looking for the best men he could find, and Kit and Owens were among them. The two men sold their farm "for about half" what it was worth and headed for Bent's Fort. Josefa went back to Taos to live with her family.

At Bent's Fort, Frémont greeted Kit with delight but without surprise, noting in his journal, "This was like Carson, prompt, self-sacrificing, and true." Among the men who had signed on for the third expedition were two of Kit's old cronies: Tom Fitzpatrick and Lucien Maxwell. Charles

Preuss, the German mapmaker, had been replaced by an American, Edward Kern of Philadelphia.

Frémont's third expedition left Bent's Fort on August 16, 1845, its leader mounted on his horse Sacramento. The journey went smoothly as the men crossed Colorado, Utah, and Nevada. When they reached the Great Salt Lake on October 13, the water level was so low that Kit, Frémont, and several others rode out to a small island. Frémont named it Antelope Island for the animals that they found there. Fresh meat was needed, so several antelope were shot. When the men got back to shore, they were scolded by an elderly Ute who said the animals rightly belonged to him. Frémont was amused but did not want to stir up trouble. He presented the old man with several tokens of good will—red cloth, a knife, and tobacco.

As the expedition prepared to cross the Mojave Desert, the hot, dry weather suggested that the journey might be as difficult as the one Kit had taken with Ewing Young years before. Rather than risk sending the whole team across the vast barren stretch, Frémont picked Kit to lead three others to search for water and grass. He instructed Kit to pick the highest point in the landscape and build a signal for the others to head toward. Kit found grass and water two days later; he built a fire on an elevation that Frémont named Pilot Peak.

In November, after camp had been made one evening along the eastern edge of the Sierra Nevadas, expedition members settled down to roast chunks of meat over a blazing fire. Afterward, the men stretched out to smoke their pipes, when suddenly Kit sat bolt upright and pointed into the darkness. Barely visible at the rim of firelight stood an old woman, poorly dressed in spite of the weather. She stumbled away, but the men surrounded her and urged her to warm herself first. Using sign language, she said she was too old and too slow to keep up with her tribe and had been left behind. Kit gave her roasted meat, assuming she might sit by the fire to eat. But she wandered back into the darkness, and no trace of her was found the next day. No one believed she would survive the coming winter.

By December 9, 1845, the expedition reached Sutter's Fort. Once again, "Captain Sutter received [us] with the same friendly hospitality which had been so delightful to us the year before," said Frémont. Then, accompanied by the American consul in California, Thomas O. Larkin, Frémont paid calls on Mexican officials—General Jose Castro, the commanding general, and Juan Alvarado, former governor of the region.

Frémont requested permission to buy food and supplies in Monterey, which "was readily granted," he reported, "and during the two days I stayed I was treated with every courtesy." By March 3, 1846, however, the welcome had cooled off as Mexican officials became suspicious about the Americans' intentions. Frémont was camped along the Salinas River 25 miles (40 kilometers) from Monterey when a letter was delivered from General Castro ordering the Americans to leave California at once.

Frémont "refused compliance to an order insulting to my government and myself." Instead he moved his camp to the crest of a hill between the Salinas and San Joaquin rivers called Gavilan Peak. Thomas Larkin warned Frémont what his refusal would cause: "In all probability [the Mexicans] will attack you," he said, adding that Frémont's action endangered innocent Americans living in the region.

Three days later Frémont boldly hoisted an American flag over a small fort he had ordered Kit and the others to build on Gavilan Peak. "We have nowise done wrong to the people or the authorities of the country [but] we will die every man of us under the flag of our country," he declared. Mexican troops watched from a distance but did not launch an attack. The matter was temporarily resolved on March 11, when Frémont broke camp and returned to Sutter's Fort, where—to John Sutter's consternation—he established a military headquarters.

On May 13, 1846, the U.S. Congress officially declared war against

A Black Mark

In April 1846, after a party of Indians was accused of harassing whites, Frémont reacted as impetuously as he had at Gavilan Peak. He gathered some of his men together, including Kit, recruited a small militia from among the American settlers, and tracked the suspects to their camp. In a three-hour slaughter, 175 Native American men, women, and children were killed. The avengers did not lose a single man, suggesting that the Indians were not armed. The incident has been compared to other slaughters committed by whites against Indians: Colorado's Sand Creek massacre of Cheyenne in 1864, Arizona's Aravaipa Creek massacre of Apache in 1871, and South Dakota's Wounded Knee massacre of Sioux in 1890. Did Frémont ever regret his actions? Perhaps, for he did not mention the event in his journals. Kit, however, called it "perfect butchery."

Mexico after General Zachary Taylor carried the American flag 119 miles (192 kilometers) into Mexican-held territory in Texas. The United States had already stationed a ship off the California coast in the event hostilities broke out in California. In July, after navy commander John

Sloat received word of the official declaration of war, he raised an American flag and asked Frémont to bring a hundred men to the coast to act as a police force.

Frémont picked an American settler, Ezekiel Merritt, as his field lieutenant and directed him to proceed to Sonoma where the Mexican Army had stored cannons, rifles, and ammunition but had stationed no soldiers to guard them. Merritt followed orders and on June 14 also seized General Guadalupe Vallejo and two officers, turning them over to Frémont. A white flag bearing the image of a grizzly bear painted on it was raised over Sonoma; ever after, the occasion was known as the Bear Flag Revolt.

When Frémont took his prisoners to Sutter's Fort, John Sutter was furious. For years he had maintained excellent relations with the Mexican government and was outraged by Frémont's highhanded tactics. Frémont—who had been treated so hospitably by Sutter—threatened his former host with severe punishment if the prisoners escaped. To prevent that from happening, Frémont put Edward Kern, his mapmaker, in charge of the captives with instructions "to shoot any person" who interfered. Frémont's behavior then grew even more unusual. He signed his dispatches "the Military Commander of U.S. Forces in California," rode at the head of his troops surrounded by bodyguards, and tied victory ribbons to Sacramento's mane and tail.

One by one, small villages along the coast, including San Diego and Los Angeles, fell like dominoes to Frémont. On July 9, the Stars and Stripes was hoisted in San Francisco. At daybreak on July 11, accompanied by a twenty-one-gun salute, Frémont raised the American flag at Sutter's Fort. Commander Robert Stockton, in charge of the ship in San Francisco Bay after Commander Sloat fell ill, appointed Frémont the military governor of the area, and the two men documented their victories in dispatches to be sent to Washington, D.C. A courier—a man known for his loyalty and ability—was needed to guarantee that the dispatches

In May 1846, war was declared against Mexico after General Zachary Taylor carried the American flag 119 miles (192 kilometers) into Mexican-held territory in Texas. Taylor later became the twelfth president of the United States.

In June 1846, John Charles Frémont ordered volunteers from among the American settlers living in California to proceed to Sonoma, where the Mexican government had stored arms and ammunition. The settlers raised a white flag painted with the image of a grizzly bear over the city. The event, known as the Bear Flag Revolt, is still celebrated every year in Sonoma.

reached their destination swiftly and were presented personally to the president. There was only one man Frémont trusted.

"On September 5, 1846, I was ordered to Washington as a bearer of dispatches," Kit said, and took with him an escort of fifteen men, including his old friend Lucien Maxwell. He was given sixty days to make the journey, which meant he needed to travel light. His party left California with only 25 pounds (11.4 kilograms) of dried meat and a few bags of *pinole*, a mixture of cornmeal and bean flour. The men pushed themselves and their animals mercilessly: several animals died along the way, while others were killed for food.

For all his dedication, though, it wasn't Kit who delivered the dispatches to Washington. By October 6, having covered 800 miles (1,288 kilometers) in 30 days, an amazing average of about 27 miles (43.5 kilometers) a day, Kit met General Stephen W. Kearny near Socorro, New Mexico. Kearny, commander of a three-hundred-man army, had strict orders from President Polk to assume control of the conquest of California. Since Kearny was a stranger in that part of the West and his own guide, Tom Fitzpatrick, was not familiar with the best route to California, he ordered Kit to guide him to his destination.

To Kearny's astonishment, Kit refused.

Kit believed he was under Frémont's command and nobody else's. "I told him I could not turn back—that I had pledged myself to . . . Frémont [and Stockton] to take their dispatches through to Washington . . . that I was under more obligations to Frémont than to any other man alive." Kearny pointed out in forceful terms that *he* was Kit's superior— Frémont's, too—and that Kit must obey the order or face charges of mutiny. Grudgingly, Kit agreed. The honor of carrying the dispatches to Washington, D.C., then fell to Tom Fitzpatrick.

During Kit's brief absence from California, events had taken an ominous turn. The Mexican Army had recaptured lost territory, including Los Angeles. When Kearny entered the struggle on December 6, 1846, his first battle took place northeast of San Diego, where thirty-six Americans died or were wounded. Kearny himself was severely injured and almost died of blood loss. Someone would have to go for reinforcements; again, Kit was picked for the job.

As chief of scouts, Kit left San Diego on December 29 with a detachment of six hundred men to help retake Los Angeles. By January 8, 1847, the troops were 15 miles (24.2 kilometers) south of the village and by January 13 had joined forces with Frémont. General Kearny,

THE WOLF WILL ESCAPE

In early December 1846, General Andres Pico had trapped the Americans in rocky, waterless territory near San Diego. When Pico learned that Kit Carson was with General Kearny, he warned his troops to take care, or "*Se escapara el lobo*—The wolf [Kit] will escape"— and would bring reinforcements from Commander Stockton in San Diego. In the middle of the night, Kit and a volunteer stuffed their moccasins into their pockets and crawled for 2 miles (3.2 kilometers) on their bellies, passing so near the enemy they could smell the Mexicans' fragrant *cigaritos*. The volunteer believed the mission was hopeless, but Kit assured him, "Providence has always saved me." But they did lose their moccasins and had to walk barefoot the rest of the way to San Diego—35 miles (56.4 kilometers)—over rocks and cacti. Stockton sent 175 soldiers, saving Kearny from certain defeat. Kit's companion, however, collapsed and did not recover for two years.

approaching from the opposite direction, ordered Frémont by courier, "Join us as soon as you can" and waited for a reply.

On January 14, 1847, without responding to the general, Frémont rode into Los Angeles with Kit at his side (it was to be the last time they rode together) to negotiate a peace agreement with General

General Stephen W. Kearny was fifty-two years old when President James K. Polk made him commander of the three-hundred-man Army of the West. Kearny was sent to California to replace John Charles Frémont and to take control of the war with Mexico.

Andres Pico. Frémont—who regarded himself, not Kearny, as the true conqueror of California—thereby claimed the victory, depriving Kearny of the right. It was an act of insubordination the general did not forget.

On February 25, Carson headed for Washington, D.C., again, this time with letters for the Benton family as well as dispatches for the U.S. Department of War. It was not an easy journey; the western frontier was hard on men and even more cruel to animals. Twenty-five years later, Lieutenant Edward F. Beale remembered "the poor mules [famished and thirsty], with their tucked flanks and dim eyes, and [heard] their sad, plaintive cry."

Kit eagerly accepted the courier's job for two reasons. He had been denied the honor by General Kearny a few months earlier, and he would have a chance to stop a day or two to see Josefa. There was no way he could know that a massacre had taken place in Taos, changing forever the lives of Josefa and her family.

SEVEN

King of the Mountain Men

On no account do I wish to forfeit the good opinion of . . . my countrymen merely because the United States Senate did not deem it proper to confirm my appointment.

—Kit Carson

Three months after Charles Bent was named governor of the newly annexed Territory of New Mexico, he heard rumors that a rebellion against American rule would take place around Christmastime. In mid-December 1846, he made a few arrests and warned his wife, Ignacia, of the possible dangers. Christmas and New Year's came and went, and when nothing happened, Bent relaxed. He removed the guards that had been placed around his house.

January 19, 1847, dawned cold and snowy. At 7:30 a.m. the Bent family was wakened by loud voices coming from the yard. Bent opened the door, half asleep, and asked the crowd of men what they wanted. "Your gringo head!" they yelled. The governor tried to calm the rebels, even as his ten-year-old son, Albert, handed him a rifle and whispered, "Papa, let us fight like men."

At the back of the house, Ignacia, Josefa, and fifteen-year-old Rumalda Boggs started to dig a hole through an adobe wall leading to an inner room. Their only tools were a large iron spoon and a poker from the fireplace, but they made an opening large enough to crawl through. At the front of the house, the mob refused to listen to Bent; he was shot and fell back, mortally wounded.

The women were able to drag the governor through the opening they had made in the wall, but he died soon afterward. Two young visitors, Josefa's brother Pablo Jaramillo and his friend Narciso Beaubien, covered themselves with hay in a loft. A servant, sympathetic to the rebels, pointed to their hiding place. "Kill the young ones," she cried, "and they will never be men to trouble us!" The boys were dragged out and hacked to death. Among several others killed in the massacre were Taos's sheriff Stephen Lee, Josefa's uncle Cornelio Vigil, and attorney J. W. Leal. Only when Kit stopped in Taos four months later on his way to Washington, D.C., did he learn what had happened. He ignored Frémont's orders to deliver the documents as quickly as possible and stayed in Taos for ten days to console Josefa and her sister as best he could.

When Kit arrived at the train station in Washington in June 1847, he was greeted by Jessie Frémont. It was their first meeting, but Jessie said she had heard so much about him from her husband that she felt as if they were old friends. Kit told Jessie he feared that people in Washington would not want anything to do with him if they knew he had had an Indian wife. She assured him that in fact people were eager to meet him. Kit—although sensitive to criticism himself—did not hesitate to remark about certain eastern gentlemen. "With their big houses and

Jessie Frémont, daughter of Senator Thomas Hart Benton, and wife of John Charles Frémont. In 1847 she met Kit Carson for the first time in Washington, D.C. She told Kit she felt as if they were already friends, because she had heard so many fine reports about him from her husband.

easy living they think they are princes," he told Jessie, "but on the plains we are the princes—they could not live there without us."

During his stay in Washington, Kit had two personal interviews with President Polk. They discussed the dispute between Frémont and General Kearny as to which man was the true conqueror of California. Kit supported his friend, but Polk noted in his diary, "I consider that Col. Fremont was greatly in the wrong when he refused to obey orders issued to him by General Kearny." Polk had no doubts about Kit, however. He was deeply impressed by the King of the Mountain Men and decided to reward him for his service to the nation. Although Congress was not in session at the time to officially approve military appointments, Polk conferred on Kit the rank of lieutenant in the Regiment of Mountain Riflemen.

When Kit returned to California in October 1847 with dispatches from the president, he discovered a far different situation than the one

KING OF THE MOUNTAIN MEN

Kit was amazed to discover on his first visit to Washington, D.C., that he was a famous man. Everyone knew who he was. He was invited to fancy parties; he was hailed as a hero wherever he went. Why? Because in 1845 the U.S. government had published ten thousand copies of Colonel John Charles Frémont's official report about his explorations in the West. In it, Frémont heaped praise on Kit's courage and bravery; newspaper reporters dubbed Carson the King of the Mountain Men, which made Lieutenant George Brewerton think he would meet someone "over six feet tall—a sort of Hercules [with] a voice like a lion." He found instead a man whose voice "was as soft and gentle as a woman's." William Tecumseh Sherman was surprised to find "a small, stoop-shouldered man, with reddish hair, freckled face, soft blue eyes, and nothing to indicate . . . courage and daring."

he had left months earlier. Colonel Richard B. Mason was the new territorial governor, and Frémont was gone. On August 22, General Kearny had arrested him on charges of mutiny and "conduct prejudicial to military discipline." On November 2, a three-month court-martial trial

Thomas Hart Benton, U.S. senator from Missouri, supported expansion of U.S. boundaries into the West. His speeches in the Senate were so fiery that he earned the name the Thunderer. Benton was bitterly disappointed that President James K. Polk sided with Kearny against Frémont. Benton never spoke to the president again.

began in Washington, D.C. Senator Thomas Hart Benton, head of the Military Affairs Committee, fiercely defended his son-in-law, but thirty-six-year-old Frémont was found guilty and resigned from the army. Another outcome of the trial: President Polk and Benton, longtime best friends, never spoke again.

Frémont's disgrace soon affected Kit. He was informed by Colonel E. W. B. Newby that his lieutenant's commission in the Regiment of Mountain Riflemen had been rejected. "The Senate of the United States did not deem it proper to confirm me on the appointment of an office that I never sought," Kit remarked. His friends urged him to quit his job as a government dispatch rider, which had included carrying news to Washington about the discovery of gold at Sutter's Mill. Kit's reply would not have surprised Frémont. "It does not matter to me whether I am enjoying the rank of lieutenant or only the credit of being an experienced mountaineer," he said. Nor had he changed his mind about Frémont, saying, "The credit he deserves I am incapable [of doing] him justice."

Gold fever never infected Kit. When his job as a dispatch rider ended, he went into partnership with Lucien Maxwell with the aim of trying his hand once again at ranching. "Now was the time, if ever, to make a home for ourselves and children." He had used similar words regarding his partnership with Dick Owens, but this time he was aware of how much Josefa had suffered when her relatives had been murdered. He did not want to leave her again. Kit and Maxwell built a two-story log cabin at Rayado, New Mexico, surrounded by an adobe wall to protect against Indian attacks. Outbuildings, corrals, stables, and a slaughterhouse were erected. New Mexico became an official U.S. territory in September 1850, and Kit's first son, William, was born two years later.

Kit's life—settled peacefully into the roles of husband, father, and rancher—was about to change in a way he could never have guessed. By January 1854, the U.S. government had assumed the responsibility of providing for the care of 350,000 Indians across the nation, who were to be supervised by 100 agents. The Apache were considered one of the most unmanageable tribes, but no white man understood them better than Kit Carson. After years of hunting and trapping in Apache country, he was familiar with their territory and their customs. He spoke their language as well as other Indian dialects. Fittingly, he was appointed the agent not only for the Apache but also for the Ute and Pueblo tribes.

Nothing Kit tackled in life—beginning the day he left Workman's saddle shop—had turned out to be easy. Soon after reporting for duty as an Indian agent on January 9, 1854, he realized it would be the most difficult job of all. He had been on the job only a month when the Apache began to steal horses and cattle from white settlers, resulting in a battle with U.S. military forces at the Red River.

Kit understood the predicament of the Apache and why they behaved as they did. The settlement of New Mexico by whites had left

KIT AND JOSEFA CARSON'S CHILDREN

Stella Carson, born December 23, 1866. When she was twenty-two years old, she married Tom Wood and became the mother of three sons and a daughter. She died in 1899, three months before her thirtieth birthday.

Rebecca Carson, born April 13, 1864, in Taos, was raised by Kit's friends, Thomas and Rumalda Boggs. Life was difficult for her, and Rebecca committed suicide when she was twenty-one years old.

William	Born October 1, 1852	Rebecca	Born April 13, 1864
Teresina	Born June 23, 1855	Stella	Born December 23, 1866
Christopher	Born June 13, 1858	Josefita	Born April 13, 1868
Charles	Born August 2, 1861		

Teresina Carson, born June 23, 1855, Kit and Josefa Carson's oldest daughter. She attended school in Lawrence, Kansas, and married DeWitt Allen in 1871. The couple had several children, all of whom died in infancy.

Josefita Carson, born April 13, 1868. Josefita never knew either of her parents, for her mother Josefa died ten days after giving birth to her and her father, Kit, died soon after. Josefita was raised by the Boggs family, as were several other Carson children.

them essentially homeless. In addition, wild game was becoming scarce. The Apache resorted to raids on settlers' homesteads as a way to feed themselves. Nevertheless, David Meriwether, the new governor of New Mexico, opted for a harsh policy toward the Indians in his district.

Kit knew that Meriwether's approach would only make matters worse. Carson went out—alone, without a military escort—to visit one of the Apache bands camped near Taos. He pointed out to the chiefs they would cause themselves and their families more grief if they did not behave peacefully. But he also had advice for his superiors: it would be best if the Indians were "sent for, and a fair and just treaty be made with them," which might help avoid unnecessary bloodshed.

William S. Messervy, acting governor while Meriwether was on temporary leave, sharply rejected Kit's opinion. "I shall listen to no terms of peace," he retorted. Instead, sixty government troops under the command of Lieutenant J. W. Davidson were sent out to punish some Apache who had fortified themselves in the Embudo Mountains 20 miles (32.2 kilometers) from Taos. Once again Kit warned, "their sufferings and privations are now very great . . . but thinking . . . there will be no mercy shown them," the Apache would resort to even more deadly measures.

After a band of Ute stole thirty head of cattle from settlers, Kit pointed out again that the Indians "are unable to support themselves by the chase and hunt . . . the government has but one alternative, either to subsist and clothe them or exterminate them." Once, Kit had been an enemy of Indian tribes himself; now, as their agent, he saw both sides of the situation. On one hand, he knew the Indians had to bow to the power of the government; on the other, the government had to accept its responsibility to the Indians.

The Ute often visited Kit in Taos at his office, calling him Father Kit. They believed they could trust him, and in September 1854 complained that "while all the Indians of the North are receiving presents,

David Meriwether, superintendent of Indian affairs for the territory of New Mexico, was Kit Carson's boss after Kit accepted the job as agent for the Apache, Ute, and Pueblo tribes. Kit, who spoke the Indians' languages, understood their side of many issues, leading to disagreement with Meriwether's often harsh policies.

they receive none." Kit reminded his superiors that winter was coming and urged the government to send blankets and coats as soon as possible. The "presents" arrived, as he had requested, but with tragic consequences. Several Indians who received them died of smallpox. The Ute believed the whites intended to wipe them out with disease and reacted swiftly. Led by one-eyed Chief Blanco, they joined the Apache in raids in northern New Mexico.

When Governor Meriwether returned from leave in July 1854, his relationship with Kit continued to be strained. He criticized Kit's competence as an agent. "Poor Kit was a good trapper, hunter, and guide," he said, but the praise he had received from his association with Frémont "had spoiled him." Indian agents often were poorly paid, and many deliberately overcharged the government in their financial reports as a means of getting extra money. Meriwether suspected Kit did the same, complaining that his bookkeeping accounts "were always wrong."

Exactly at Two O'Clock

On May 23, 1854, Kit accompanied Major James H. Carleton in pursuit of a band of Apache. After following their trail through narrow ravines and steep mountain passes for six days, Kit estimated they would find the Indians at around two o'clock the next afternoon. Major Carleton scoffed at Kit's prediction and said he'd buy him the finest hat made in New York if Kit turned out to be right. At exactly two o'clock the following day, "The Indians were found at the hour I had predicted," Kit said. "The major fulfilled his promise presenting to me a hat . . . a fine one it was." On the hatband were embroidered the words

At two-o'clock,
Kit Carson from Major Carleton

Indeed Kit realized he was handicapped by illiteracy and needed a clerk to whom he could dictate letters and reports. He noted on August 31, 1858, "I have in my employ . . . John Mostin . . . aged 29 years, at a salary of $500 per year." When he billed the government for Mostin's services, however, Meriwether objected to the "charges for . . . $13 when I am ignorant of any regulations which authorize an Agent to have a clerk." Thereafter, Kit paid the clerk out of his own pocket and later dictated his life story to Mostin.

Kit Carson in 1854, when the U.S. government appointed him as the agent of three southwestern tribes. He was forty-five years old and brought the same dedication to his post as he did to trapping, exploring, and raising a family.

In spite of Meriwether's complaints, when Kit's first term as an agent expired he was reappointed to a second term, then for a third. In 1860 Kit went with several friends on a hunting trip in the San Juan Mountains. As he led his horse along a steep hillside—with a rope around the animal's neck so he could let go quickly if the horse fell—the horse tumbled down the slope. Kit got tangled in the rope and was dragged along, spraining his shoulder and severely bruising his chest.

Kit had suffered injuries before, however, and didn't complain. Besides, he had much on his mind: Josefa's newest pregnancy, persistent problems with the tribes he oversaw, rumors about a war brewing in the East. If the conflict came to pass, it would pit North against South, American against American.

EIGHT

Death at Fort Lyon

We must convince [the Indians] by our treatment of them of the kind intentions of the Government, otherwise I fear that they will lose confidence in our promises.

—Kit Carson

In November 1860, Abraham Lincoln was elected the sixteenth president of the United States as the nation debated the issue of slavery. Was it compatible with democracy? Lincoln believed it was not.

On December 20, South Carolina seceded from the Union. Soon after, the Confederate States of America was founded when six other Southern states that depended on slavery also left the Union. A war between the North and South—the Civil War—commenced on April 12, 1861, when Confederate troops fired on Fort Sumter, a Union supply depot in South Carolina. Three days later, Lincoln called for 75,000 volunteers to put down the rebellion.

Kit, Southern by birth, might have been expected to side with the South. But he believed in preserving the Union, and when Southern sympathizers tried to hoist a Confederate flag in the plaza in Taos, he nailed an American flag to a cottonwood pole and posted a twenty-four-hour guard to make sure it was not pulled down. Two months later, Kit resigned his post as Indian agent and was named commander of the First New Mexico Volunteers.

Although it seemed unlikely that a war over slavery would extend into New Mexico, Confederate troops tried to stir up the southwestern tribes—Apache, Kiowa, Ute, and Navajo—and pit them against the Union. On February 21, 1862, Carson's volunteers joined ranks with Colonel Edward Canby to face General Henry Sibley's Confederates in the Battle of Valverde along the Rio Grande.

The battle began in the morning, as Union forces crossed the river to attack the enemy. Carson and his men fought beside the Colorado Volunteers, whose red-striped gray shirts made them easy targets. By sunset it was clear the Confederates had won. Canby lost 68 men, with 157 wounded and 34 missing in action. In spite of their early defeat, however, Canby's forces drove the Confederates out of New Mexico a month later and claimed it for the Union.

The Southwest had been saved from the Confederates, but the threat from the angry Indian tribes remained. In May 1862, Kit and his five companies headed to Fort Stanton, commanded by James H. Carleton (now a general, who several years earlier had given Kit a fine hat), with orders to take action against Apache who were attacking settlers and stealing livestock. Carleton's solution to the Apache problem was chilling: "All Indian men . . . are to be killed whenever and wherever you can find them."

What did Kit think of such orders? His job as an Indian agent meant he acted as a caretaker, not a killer. His response to Carleton's order spoke louder than words: Indian men were not arbitrarily killed but were taken captive instead. Within weeks after the campaign started, he had rounded up more than five hundred men, women, and children. It was true that Kit had fought hard against Blackfeet and Sioux during the 1830s, but in his view the plight of the southwestern tribes in the 1860s was far different. Chief Cadete of the Mescalero Apache eloquently summed up the Indians' dilemma in a surrender speech.

> *We are worn out; we have no more heart; we have no provisions, no means to live; your troops are everywhere; our springs and water holes are occupied by your young men. You have driven us from our last and best stronghold. . . . Do with us as may seem good to you, but do not forget we are men and brave.*

The Confederates had been driven out of New Mexico; threats from the Apache were quelled for the moment. Kit concluded that his obligation as a volunteer had been fulfilled. On February 2, 1863, he notified General Carleton that he intended to return to his family in Taos. Carleton urged Kit

General James H. Carleton was ordered by the U.S. government in 1862 to take action against Indian tribes in the Southwest that were attacking white settlers and stealing livestock. With Kit Carson's help, he finally subdued the Navajo, the largest and most financially successful of the tribes.

to reconsider, because the Apache were not the only tribe that needed to be dealt with. To ease his mind about his family's welfare, Carleton offered Kit a two-month leave of absence.

On April 11, as Kit was about to return to duty, Carleton requested that he hire ten Ute Indians and four Mexican guides who were familiar with Navajo country. Carleton planned to lead a thousand troops into the land of red-rock canyons. The Navajo, the largest and wealthiest of the southwestern tribes, still ranged freely over a 25,000-square-mile (64,750 square-kilometer) area. They were skilled farmers and keepers of livestock, were able to provide for their families, and refused to yield to American rule.

The military campaign against the Navajo began on July 7, 1863, when Carson and his men arrived at Fort Defiance in Arizona Territory. Carleton's decision to go after the Navajo was one thing; finding them was another. The Navajo knew their homeland better than any white man and vanished into the red-walled canyons like ghosts. The troops seized Navajo livestock, but couldn't always hang on to the animals. After a large herd of sheep was captured in October 1863, a grazing camp in a steep-walled canyon was set up to hold the animals. An officer was put in charge of the flock, but on the morning of October 26 he woke to find the Navajo had recaptured many of their animals. Not content with taking back their own livestock, they also had driven off forty-eight mules and eight oxen belonging to the army.

All the while, Kit had not felt himself since his tumble down the rocky hillside three years earlier. Chest pain and shortness of breath were troublesome; he asked for a second leave, hoping a rest would help him recover. General Carleton refused the request and ordered him to proceed into the Canyon de Chelly, a suspected Navajo sanctuary. If Kit brought in a hundred captives, Carleton promised, he could take the leave he had asked for. Kit was "satisfied there are very few Indians" in the canyon, but an order was an order. In August 1863,

Kit Carson in 1866, two years before his death. Even as his health declined, he never lost his composure and looked on the world with the same penetrating, no-nonsense gaze.

with a company of 350 men he proceeded toward Canyon de Chelly.

As Kit moved his troops toward the canyon, he ordered the systematic destruction of 350 acres (142 hectares) of corn, as well as fields of wheat, pumpkins, beans, and melons. Hundreds of sheep were rounded up and shot, their carcasses left to rot in the blazing sun. By Kit's calculation, "some two or three thousand peach trees" were also destroyed. Every Navajo dwelling that was found was burned to the ground. Although the Navajo themselves remained elusive, Kit knew there was one enemy they could not hide from: starvation.

Heavy snow fell shortly before Kit's troops entered the western entrance of the Canyon de Chelly on January 6, 1864. A few Navajo were sighted but vanished into a branching canyon so narrow it looked like "a place where nothing save an Indian or a mountain goat" could make its way. Now Kit's strategy produced results: without food, without proper shelter, and assaulted by freezing weather, small groups of Navajo began to surrender. One group of fourteen women and children had survived for weeks on only piñon nuts. Kit had not believed he could meet Carleton's order to capture one hundred Indians, but by January 24 more than five hundred had surrendered. Carleton kept his promise, and Kit returned briefly to Taos.

By February so many Navajo—about 1,500—had surrendered that insufficient provisions were available, and many died at Fort Defiance. Carleton miscalculated the total Navajo population at 5,000; in 1860 it actually numbered about 14,000. After an additional eight hundred Navajo turned themselves in, food supplies ran so low that, in spite of Kit's protest, Carleton ordered their meager rations reduced even further.

It became clear that a new fort was needed to assume responsibility for the large numbers of homeless Navajo who had been added to the many Apache who had already surrendered. About 140 miles (225 kilometers) southeast of Santa Fe, the Pecos River flowed across the flat plain and around a circular stand of cottonwood trees. The Spanish called the site Bosque Redondo, or "Round Grove." General Carleton chose it as a reservation for the two tribes and work commenced on Fort Sumner.

In July 1864, Kit was appointed superintendent of nine thousand Indians held at the fort—a combination of seven thousand Navaho and two thousand Apache—two tribes that were long-standing rivals, making peacekeeping difficult. Even so, in their first year at Fort Sumner, the Navajo planted hundreds of acres of corn that appeared to be doing well. Sadly, the entire crop became infested with corn-boring worms, leaving the husks empty. The next year more corn was planted. This time, the crop did well until the Pecos River flooded the fields during the spring rains. The third year the Indians refused to plant a crop.

So many Navajo and Apache surrendered to General Carleton that a larger fort had to be built to accommodate their needs. Carleton chose a site 140 miles (225 kilometers) from Santa Fe to build Fort Sumner. Kit Carson was placed in charge of it.

On June 1, 1868, a treaty was signed with the Navajo giving them a reservation on a portion of their old tribal lands. They were given seeds, farm implements, and flocks of sheep and goats. On June 18, in a column 10 miles (16 kilometers) long, escorted by four companies of U.S. cavalry, 7,000 Navajo headed to a new reservation 400 miles (644 kilometers) to the west. Many who had survived starvation and disease at Fort Sumner died during the journey. One officer reported that of the 950 Navajo he escorted, 110 died—more than 10 percent. Kit had not ordered the march, but he became a symbol of evil among the Navajo that persists to the present day. He is remembered for the scorched-earth policy that destroyed their homes, fields, and livestock, and is blamed for what the Navajo call the Long Walk.

Kit's men noticed he was still exhausted after returning from his second leave, yet Carleton had another assignment for him. On November 10, 1864, a campaign was launched against the Kiowa and Comanche. The Plains tribes had gone on a rampage, attacking wagon trains, killing settlers, and taking captives—including five young brothers from one family. The Indians viewed their actions as justified: they had agreed to let whites use the Sante Fe Trail if they promised not to stray from it. When the whites did, the Indians resorted to their own brand of revenge.

At sundown on November 24, as Kit was camped at Mule Creek, Indian scouts returned with news that they had picked up the enemy's trail. Kit ordered his men—13 officers, 246 troops, and 75 Ute and Apache warriors—to prepare for a night march. At dawn the following day, Kit's men found Kiowa and Comanche numbering in the thousands near an abandoned fort called Adobe Walls.

Realizing he was badly outnumbered, Kit knew he had no chance in a fight with the Indians. He settled for destroying their village—tipis were burned along with buffalo robes, clothing, and food supplies—making the approaching winter difficult. As a result, the Kiowa and Comanche bargained for peace the following year. Kit's cautious behavior at Adobe Walls saved him from the kind of miscalculation made by General George Custer twelve years later. (When Custer came upon a similar large encampment of Sioux and Cheyenne at the Little Big Horn River in Montana, he attacked, losing his life and the lives of his entire command.) Two months after Adobe Walls, General Carleton praised Kit, saying that the battle added "another green leaf to the laurel wreath which you have so nobly won in the service of your country." On March 13, 1865, Kit was commissioned a brigadier general, an appointment he accepted despite being denied his lieutenant's commission in 1847.

Kit retired from the army in November 1867 but, regardless of his failing health, he still needed an income to support his growing family.

He was appointed the agent for three small bands of Ute and Apache at Fort Garland in southern Colorado. Josefa and the children moved with him, yet Kit's health worsened steadily. He grew so weak that he traveled everywhere by wagon and finally consulted Dr. H. R. Tilton, a surgeon at nearby Fort Lyon. Dr. Tilton offered little hope of a cure.

When the U.S. Congress established a commission to study the Ute situation, Kit made it clear that he believed a reservation set aside for each of the various Indian tribes was the only hope for peace. Referring to the Ute, he said, "They are a brave, warlike people [but] they cannot live much longer as now." Further bloodshed was likely, he added, if their lives were not improved.

In January 1868, Kit was asked to accompany the Ute chiefs to Washington, D.C., to discuss a new treaty settlement that would resolve their grievances against the government. Josefa was expecting a seventh child, but urged him to make the trip because it would give him a chance to seek medical advice about the pains in his chest. In March a new settlement was agreed on, giving the Ute 15,120,000 acres (6.1 million hectares) in western Colorado with promises from the government that no one could "enter, reside, pass over, or settle" there except the Ute. (The ink on the contract was barely dry before white settlers violated it.)

Kit was examined by doctors in New York, Philadelphia, and Boston. They all told him the same thing: there was no remedy for his ailment, diagnosed as an aortic aneurysm, an enlargement of a section of the aorta, the heart's main blood vessel. Realizing his time was growing short, Kit posed for a final photograph before leaving Boston. When he arrived home on April 11, he found it even more difficult to breathe. On April 13, 1868, Josefa delivered their seventh child—a daughter, Josefita—but died two weeks later.

His wife's death, after twenty-five years of marriage, hastened Kit's own end. He arranged for a nurse to care for his newborn child, asked

In January 1868, Kit accompanied a delegation representing the Ute tribe to Washington, D.C, to help negotiate a treaty with the U.S. government. While in the capital, the famous Civil War photographer Mathew Brady made a portrait of Kit and three other members of the delegation. Kit died five months later, on May 14, 1868, at Fort Lyon, Colorado.

Josefa's sister Ignacia to come from Taos to care for the other children, and made out a will, with instructions "to have my own body . . . and that of my wife" returned to Taos for burial. Then he calmly faced death.

On May 14, Dr. Tilton moved fifty-eight-year-old Kit to Fort Lyon, where he could keep a closer eye on him. As the pressure of the aneurysm against his esophagus caused Kit increasing pain, the doctor administered brief whiffs of chloroform to relieve it. Because it was hard for Kit to swallow, Dr. Tilton restricted his patient's diet to soft foods, no coffee, and no tobacco. On the afternoon of May 23, however, a month after Josefa's death, Kit asked for the kind of meal he

Kit Carson requested that he and his wife Josefa be buried in Taos, the town Kit had called home for forty-two years. In 1908 a marble marker was placed at Kit's final resting place, and the cemetery is now included in the Kit Carson Memorial Park. The couple's former home in Taos has become a museum.

enjoyed—buffalo steak and hot coffee—then settled back to smoke his pipe while he chatted with the doctor. About 4:25 p.m. he suddenly exclaimed, "Doctor! Compadre! Adios!"

More than a year passed before Kit and Josefa's bodies, buried first at Fort Garland in Colorado, were taken to the cemetery in Taos. Nearby was the grave of Kit's good friend Charles Bent. Today the site is included in the Kit Carson Memorial Park. Critics—the Navajo in particular—have not spared Kit regarding his treatment of Indians. Yet, as Kit admitted himself, "I do not know whether I done right or wrong, but I done what I thought was best."

Today Kit's name survives throughout the West that he explored and knew so well. Kit Carson Highway crosses part of New Mexico and

Colorado; atop the Pioneer Monument in Denver is a statue of Kit mounted on a prancing horse. Carson City is the capital of Nevada. Fort Carson, in Colorado Springs, is an important U.S. military base. Carson Pass in the Sierra Nevadas is in tribute of the trek Kit and Frémont made to California. Inscribed on the U.S. Federal Building in Santa Fe are four words that best describe the legacy of a fifteen-year-old boy who heard "so many tales of life in the mountains" that he ran away from a saddle shop to take part in the great adventure:

He led the way.

KIT CARSON AND HIS TIMES

1720   Alexander Carson, Kit's great-grandfather, leaves Bradninch, England, and emigrates to Pennsylvania.

1761   William Carson, Kit's grandfather, moves west to Virginia's Shenandoah Valley.

1809   Kit Carson is born at Tate's Creek, Kentucky; Abraham Lincoln is born the same year, also in Kentucky.

1811   Kit's family follows Daniel Boone west to Missouri.

1818   Kit's father, Lindsey, dies while clearing land.

1822   William Becknell takes the first trade caravan down the Santa Fe Trail.

1824   Kit is apprenticed to David Workman, saddle maker, in Franklin, Missouri.

1826   Kit runs away and heads down Santa Fe Trail.

1829   Charles and William Bent establish a trading post in Colorado; Kit goes to California with Ewing Young.

1835   Kit marries an Arapaho girl, Waanibe ("Singing Grass"); he gives her an American name, Alice.

1837   Kit's daughter Adaline is born; Alice dies after the birth of their second daughter.

1842   John Charles Frémont is commissioned to map part of the unexplored lands in the West; he hires Kit as a guide.

1843   Kit marries Maria Josefa Jaramillo in Taos; he guides Frémont on a second expedition.

1845   Congress votes to extend U.S. boundaries to include west Texas and California; Kit accompanies Frémont on a third expedition.

1847   Charles Bent, governor of New Mexico, is killed in a massacre in Taos; Kit delivers military messages to Washington, D.C.

1854   Kit becomes an agent for the Apache, Ute, and Pueblo in Taos.

1858   Kit hires a clerk, John Mostin, and dictates his life story to him.

1860   Kit is injured when dragged by a horse; Abraham Lincoln is elected sixteenth president of the United States.

1863   Kit joins General James H. Carleton to subdue the Apache tribes; Navajo crops, orchards, and livestock are destroyed.

1864   Kit is named the superintendent of Fort Sumner's Navajo and Apache Indians; he is victorious at Adobe Walls.

1867   Kit retires from the army and becomes an agent for the Ute and Apache at Fort Garland, Colorado.

1868   Josefa Carson dies after the birth of her seventh child; Kit dies one month later.

1905   Kit's long-lost memoir is found in Paris; today it is owned by the Newberry Library in Chicago.

1926   Kit's memoir is published in Taos, New Mexico.

Further Research

Books

Christian, Mary Blount. *Who'd Believe John Colter?* New York: Macmillan, 1993.

Garst, Shannon. *Kit Carson: Trailblazer and Scout.* New York: Julian Messner, 1942.

Lavender, David. *The Santa Fe Trail.* New York: Holiday House, 1995.

Web Sites

Kit Carson

http://en.wikipedia.org

Kit Carson: American Hero

http://www.thehistorynet.com

Kit Carson: Guide, Trapper, Soldier, Indian Agent, and Frontiersman

http://www.virtualology.com

Kit Carson Museum on the Santa Fe Trail

http://www.santafetrailscenicandhistoricbyway.org

BIBLIOGRAPHY

Brewerton, George Douglas. *Overland with Kit Carson.* Lincoln, NE: University of Nebraska Press, 1993.

Burdett, Charles. *The Life of Kit Carson.* New York: Grossett & Dunlap, 1902.

Dary, David. *The Santa Fe Trail: Its History, Legends, and Lore.* New York: Alfred A. Knopf, 2000.

Dunlay, Tom. *Kit Carson and the Indians.* Lincoln, NE: University of Nebraska Press, 2000.

Estergreen, M. Morgan. *Kit Carson: Portrait in Courage.* Norman, OK: University of Oklahoma Press, 1962.

Gerson, Noel B. *Kit Carson: Folk Hero and Man.* New York: Doubleday, 1964.

Grant, Blanche C. *Kit Carson's Own Story of His Life.* Taos, NM: Santa Fe New Mexico Publishing Corp., 1926.

Guild, Thelma S., and Harvey L. Carter. *Kit Carson: A Pattern for Heroes.* Lincoln, NE: University of Nebraska Press, 1984.

Hicks, John D., George E. Mowry, and Robert E. Burke. *A History of American Democracy.* Boston: Houghton Mifflin, 1966.

Josephy, Alvin M., Jr. *The Great West.* New York: American Heritage, 1965.

Milner, Clyde A., II, Carol A. O'Connor, and Martha A. Sandweiss, eds. *Oxford History of the American West.* New York: Oxford University Press, 1994.

Quaife, Milo Milton, ed. *Kit Carson's Autobiography.* Lincoln, NE: University of Nebraska Press, 1966.

Roberts, David. *A Newer World: Kit Carson, John C. Frémont, and the Claiming of the American West.* New York: Simon & Schuster, 2000.

Ruth, Kent. *Great Day in the West: Forts, Posts, and Rendezvous beyond the Mississippi.* Norman: University of Oklahoma Press, 1963.

Sabin, Edwin L. *Kit Carson Days 1809–1868.* Vols. I and II. New York: Press of the Pioneers, 1935.

Bibliography

Time-Life Books. *Settling the West.* Alexandria, VA: Time-Life, 1996.

Unruh, John D., Jr. *The Plains Across: The Overland Emigrants and the Trans-Mississippi West, 1840-60.* Urbana: University of Illinois Press, 1982.

Uschan, Michael V. *Westward Expansion.* San Diego: Lucent, 2001.

Vestal, Stanley. *Kit Carson: The Happy Warrior of the Old West.* New York: Houghton Mifflin, 1928.

Viola, Herman J. *Exploring the West.* Washington, D.C.: Smithsonian Books, 1987.

INDEX

Page numbers in **boldface** are illustrations.